21st Century
Basic Skills
Library

LET'S SORT SHAPES

by Lauren Coss

Cherry Lake Publishing • Ann Arbor, Michigan

2

CHERRY
LAKE
Publishing

Published in the United States of America
by Cherry Lake Publishing
Ann Arbor, Michigan
www.cherrylakepublishing.com

Consultant: Marla Conn, ReadAbility, Inc.
Editorial direction and book production: Red Line Editorial
Book design and illustration: Design Lab

Photo Credits: Mikhail Rulkov/Shutterstock Images, cover, 1; Channarong Meesuk/
Shutterstock Images, 4; Anita Potter/Shutterstock Images, 6; Red Line Editorial, 8; Jorg
Hackemann/Shutterstock Images, 10; Fuse/Thinkstock, 12; Iakov Filimonov/Shutterstock
Images, 14 (top); Kues/Shutterstock Images, 14 (bottom); moodboard/Thinkstock, 16; Markus
Mainka/Shutterstock Images, 18 (top); iStock/Thinkstock, 18 (bottom), 20 (beach ball);
photastic/Shutterstock Images, 20 (basketball), 20 (tennis ball); Voronin76/Shutterstock
Images, 20 (block); Sergio Stakhnyk/Shutterstock Images, 20 (aluminum can); Mega
Pixel/Shutterstock Images, 20 (box); YellowPixel/Shutterstock Images, 20 (dice); Givaga/
Shutterstock Images, 20 (olive jar); Evgeny Karandaev/Shutterstock Images, 20 (soda can)

Library of Congress Cataloging-in-Publication Data
Coss, Lauren, author.
  Let's sort shapes / by Lauren Coss ; consultant: Marla Conn, ReadAbility, Inc.
     pages cm. -- (Sorting)
  Audience: Age 6.
  Audience: Grades K to 3.
  Includes index.
  ISBN 978-1-63137-632-0 (hardcover) -- ISBN 978-1-63137-677-1 (pbk.) -- ISBN 978-1-63137-
722-8 (pdf ebook) -- ISBN 978-1-63137-767-9 (hosted ebook)
 1. Shapes--Juvenile literature. 2. Set theory--Juvenile literature. I. Title. II. Title: Let us sort
shapes.

  QA445.5.C68 2014
  516--dc23
                                    2014004570

Cherry Lake Publishing would like to acknowledge the work of The Partnership for
21st Century Skills. Please visit www.p21.org for more information.

Printed in the United States of America
Corporate Graphics Inc.
July 2014

TABLE OF CONTENTS

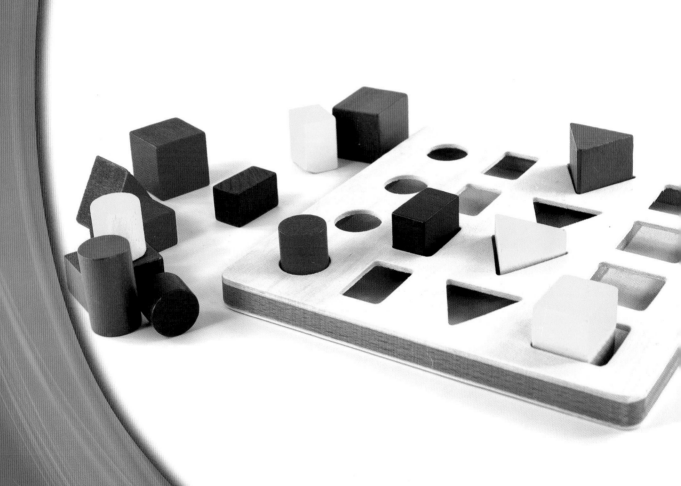

What Is Sorting?

Sorting means putting alike things into groups.

Let's try sorting shapes!

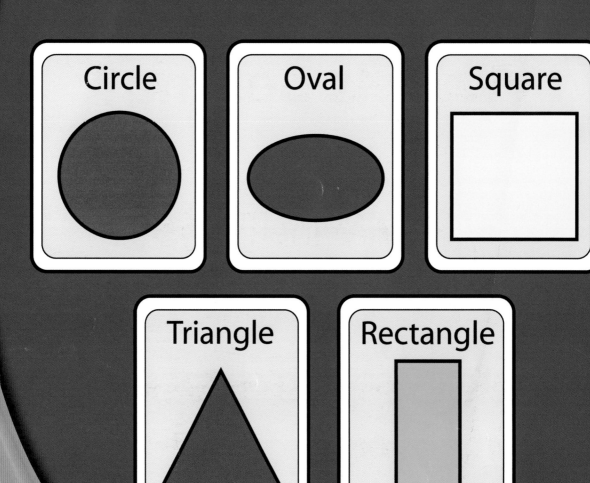

Circle

Oval

Square

Triangle

Rectangle

Flat Shapes

Shapes are the forms of things.

Some shapes are **two-dimensional**.

They are flat.

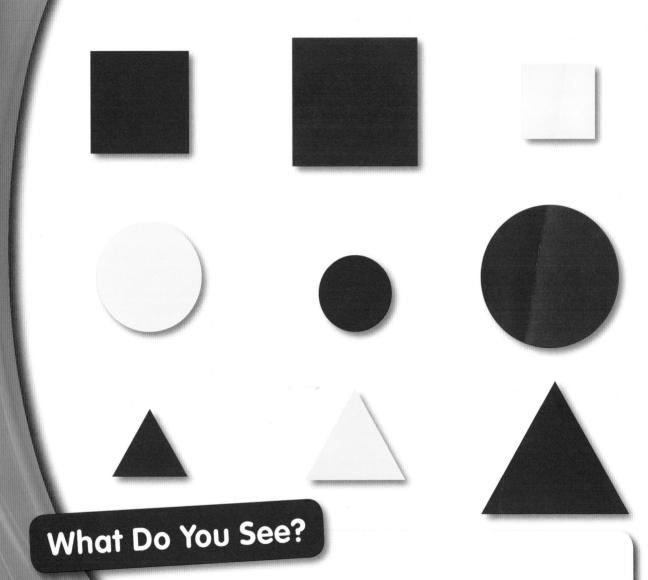

What Do You See?

How many sides does a square have?

Circles and squares are flat. So are triangles.

We can sort flat shapes by how they look.

Triangles have three sides.

Let's sort circles into a group.

One shape doesn't belong.

Why is the square **different**?

Real-Life Shapes

Some shapes are **three-dimensional**.

They are not flat.

Jess's toys are shaped like this.

What Do You See?

What colors are Jess's blocks?

Jess sorts her toys by shape.

Blocks are shaped like **cubes**.

Marbles are shaped like **spheres**.

Store Shapes

Zach sorts shapes at the store.

What shapes do you see?

Jars are **cylinders**.

Zach sorts them into a group.

Cones go in a different group.

What Do You See?

How many objects can you count in this picture?

What shapes are on this page?

How can you sort them?

Find Out More

BOOK

Cohen, Marina. *3-D Shapes*. New York: Crabtree, 2011.

WEB SITE

Curious George: I Love Shapes

pbskids.org/curiousgeorge/games/i_love_shapes/i_love_shapes.html

Help George sort the shapes. You'll have to be quick!

Glossary

cones (KOHNS) shapes with a round base on one end and a point on the other end

cubes (KYOOBS) shapes with six square sides

cylinders (SIL-uhn-durs) shapes with flat, circular ends and curved sides

different (DIF-ur-uhnt) not the same

spheres (SFEERS) shapes that are perfectly round balls

three-dimensional (THREE duh-MEN-shuh-nuhl) having length, width, and height

two-dimensional (TOO duh-MEN-shuh-nuhl) having length and width

Home and School Connection

Use this list of words from the book to help your child become a better reader. Word games and writing activities can help beginning readers reinforce literacy skills.

alike	flat	shapes	three-
blocks	forms	sides	dimensional
circles	group	sort	toys
colors	jars	spheres	triangles
cones	marbles	square	two-
cubes	objects	store	dimensional
cylinders	page	things	
different			

What Do You See?

What Do You See? is a feature paired with select photos in this book. It encourages young readers to interact with visual images in order to build the ability to integrate content in various media formats.

You can help your child further evaluate photos in this book with additional activities. Look at the images in the book without the What Do You See? feature. Ask your child to describe one detail in each image, such as a color, activity, or setting.

Index

About the Author

Lauren Coss is an author and editor who lives in Minnesota. She loves running, cross-country skiing, and gardening.